Mirror of the Soul

DAN M. KHANNA

Copyright © 2015 Dan M. Khanna

All rights reserved.

ISBN: 0692374922
ISBN-13: 978-0692374924

DEDICATION

To Tata and Maa

Tokershibhai and Narabadaben

For their selfless love, devotion and loving me as their own son.

" An unexamined life is not worth living."

Socrates

SPECIAL ACKNOWLEDGEMENT

My sincere gratitude to the management and staff of Outback Steakhouse Restaurant in San Angelo, Texas, for their hospitality and providing me an ambience and corner space where I could write hundreds of poems through many years, along with excellent food and service.

Dan Khanna

CONTENTS

Prologue

My Love	1
The Illusion of Happiness	2
The Love of My Life	3
A Sad End	5
The Journey of Life	6
The Love of Life	8
Up and Down	9
Life's Health	11
The World in My Arms	13
Love is Forever	14
Old Age	15
By My Side	17
The Presence	18
The Sheets	19
The Touch	23
The Last Lap	24
My Anchor	26
Lost My Chance	27
Love of My Life	28
The Future is the Past	30
I am Back	31
Suffering From Myself	32
Touching Happiness	33
A Broken Vessel	34
The Book of Mistakes	35
The Love Feast	37
The Feast of Love	42
The Demons Inside Me	49
Dare to Dream	51
Kismet is Dead	53
The Grind of Life	54
Selling the Soul	55
The Robotic Life	56

Together Yet Alone	57
The Dying Breed	58
The Broken Heart	59
The Final Spark	60
The Emotional Rape	61
Life Left in Me	62
The Other Side of Love	63
The Luckless Luck	64
The Mind of a Terrorist	66
Love Among the Ruins	68
The Curse of the Past	69
The Heart and Me	70
My Luck	71
Without Love	72
A Perfect Loser	73
I Feel Unclean	74
Self-Inflicted Wounds	75
The Divine Blows	76
I am Not the Right Person	77
The Prisoner of Self	79
Rich and Poor	81
The Temple of Sins	82
I Miss Life	84
As Time Goes By	85
A Loveless Life	87
The Fabric of the Heart	88
Let the Torch Pass	89
The Lone Ranger	90
The Disease of Loneliness	91
The Loser's Paradise	93
Broken Promises	94
The Wrong Train	95
The Crossroads of Life	97
The Corrupted Mind	98
The Lost Soul	99
My Mind is My Enemy	100
I am an Island	101
The Wounds of Love	102
Overcoming Myself	103
The Broken Hope	104
Life Ends	105

The End of an Affair 107
The Vanishing Intellect 108

PROLOGUE

What do we really see when we look in the mirror? Do we see ourselves? Our images? Our mirages?

But what about our inner selves? What are we?

We live our lives. We experience life. We observe life. We feel life. What do we learn?

Our thoughts float and flitter through space and time as we search within us.

There is a philosopher in all of us. Our hearts experience myriads of emotions. Our minds form images of the world around us - love, romance, intimacy, struggles, ups and downs, as we try to fathom our souls. We are the mirrors of our souls.

Dan Khanna

January 20, 2015

MY LOVE

You are my love
My one and only love
From the first time I saw you
I knew I was in love
Love, a feeling
That emerges from within
To engulf mind and body.

I knew I was in love
When you brushed against me
When you touched me
It was electric
It was natural
As if our bodies were
Made for each other
Then we kissed
And our love was complete
The kiss
The touch
The holding
Our bodies and minds
Intertwined with love and emotions
Embracing a future
That was going to be ours
A future
Where love is pure
And everlasting
And two bodies and souls
Become one
To journey together
In the heart of God
To be one soul.
You are my love.
You are my soul.

THE ILLUSION OF HAPPINESS

The illusion of happiness
Is a dangerous mirage
That feels like an oasis
Yet it is a barren desert
Ready to swallow you
In its quicksand
While you cling
To an image of
Paradise
That exists only
In your mind
While the reality hits you
Like a jackhammer
Bringing you to your senses
That happiness is just a dream
It does happen
When it does
But mostly
Happiness is just an illusion.

THE LOVE OF MY LIFE

The love of my life
Has moist lips
Gentle hands
Tender touch
And a smile
That brightens my life.

The love of my life
Holds me together
In her warm embrace
With searching touches
That caress
The emotions
To make me come alive.

The love of my life
Kisses me
With quivering lips
Igniting passion
That envelops
The entire body
And makes me whole.

The love of my life
Loves me
With yielding passion
Probing depths
That are unreachable
Exploring emotions
And unleashing feelings
That could swallow
The entire universe.

That is my love
Love that makes me complete
And makes me a person
That is worthy of her love.

She is and will remain
The love of my life.

A SAD END

It is going to be
A sad end
To a sad life
That started
With a blast
But then went downhill
The follies
The mistakes
The errors
Of judgment
The misfortune
Of luck
The disappearing
Friends and companions
Creating a lonely circle
That slowly shrinks
To crush me
Like a dark hole
Wiping my existence
To create a finality
To a sad end.

THE JOURNEY OF LIFE

The journey of life
Is a dangerous journey
Full of perils
That challenges our wits
To endure the upcoming
Battle of life
We win
We lose
Does it matter?
For we do need to live
No matter what
We do our best
Is life fair?
Yes and no
Yes
For it gives us a chance
No
For not all is fair
But we have to accept
Its frivolities
And live with its consequences
Can we do better?
Can we excel?
Yes, we can
But all is not in our control
Time is time
Fate is fate

Destiny is destiny
So what can humans do?
The best as one can
Make the effort
With sincerity and devotion
Will the journey be better?

Yes, for life is a journey
There is no destination
No end
Just a journey
The journey of life.

THE LOVE OF LIFE

The love of life
Is a gift
Given by God
That propels you
To accept life
As divine
With a purpose
To make it
The way you want to
Some do some don't
Is that destiny?
Life is love
Love it
For it is yours
You have to live it
Love your life
And live with
Passion and virtue
For you are love.

UP AND DOWN

When I was up
I looked down to see
Where I can wind up
And then it happens
I am down
Looking up
To where I want to be
Where I should be
The top
Pinnacle of success
So I start the climb
Slowly but surely
I climb up
And get there
To behold the view
Of ecstasy and pride
I look down
To laugh
Think
I will not be down again
And then I slip
I slide
Slowly at first
Picking up speed
As I head to the bottom
Hoping to crash
Down to earth
Without pride
With humility
To stare at the earth
From where I came
Shaken and stunned

I look up
Up to top
With shattered dreams
I start to crawl
Towards the top
Up to where I want to be
Up to be where I should be
To up, to down
Just like my life.

LIFE'S HEALTH

The health of my life
Is shaky and sad
The body takes on
Beatings
That slowly chip away at life
Hemorrhage, stroke, cancer
Each with its own deadliness
Able to slay the human
Yet I face
Its onslaught
Its tirade
The yearly rituals with fatality
That strengthens me
And forces me to be strong
To face the next storm
That is thrown my way
To fight the evil
That surrounds me
Smother me
And quiet me
Into oblivion
But, I won't go
Though my eyes
Lose some of their glow
My music
Loses some of my muse
But, I live with
My handicaps
For life is always a handicap
We do the best we can
But life will
Never
Extinguish me

For my strength
Is in survival
To beat life
At its own game
My health is me
My life is mine
My life's health
Is within me
And that is me.

THE WORLD IN MY ARMS

When I hold you
I feel the world
In my embrace
As if
What I wanted
In this life
Was with me
In me
I am complete
Devoid of any desire
For all desires
Fulfilled
Lay in my arms
Content and peaceful
Touching the soul
That unites us
Into a universe
Of our own
With all its beauty
Serenity and calmness
Mystery and love
When I have you
In my arms.

LOVE IS FOREVER

My love for you
Transgresses eternity
Into a time
That has no ending
It transports
Into many lifetimes
Where our souls are intermingled
Into one body
That travels together
Into space
Through heavenly bodies
Seeing colors and visions
That only we share
Only we experience
The journey is forever
It never ends
It goes on
To the heart of God
For our love
Is immortal
Is forever.

OLD AGE

Old age
Creeps up on you
When you least expect it.
Life is moving
Slowly but surely
Then suddenly
You hit, skid
And land on
The old side of life
The past becomes a blur
And the end
A grasp away
The memories of the past
Excite you
The dreams of the future
Beckon you
The body
Creaks of aches and pain
Minor hurts linger
Romance becomes an illusion
Desire is not dead
But desires
Remain desires
Become fantasy
The visits to doctors
A regular schedule
Testing and prodding
A dying life
To keep it alive
When the body's
Will to live has died

But even in old age
There is value
There is wisdom
But, it is still
Old age
Nearer to the end
And gasping for last
Straws of happiness
That may never come
Wishing for the past
That will never return
And hoping
That end comes
Soon and peacefully
And an end
That I can be proud of
I lived
Brought happiness to few
And then close the book
That gets re-shelved
Into a collection
Of classics
That may someday
Enlighten someone.
Yes, it is an old age
An age when the world becomes one
A unified vision
The old age.

BY MY SIDE

By my side
Is that side
That is all around me
It is not just one side
But it is all sides
Around me
Where you are
On all my sides
Touching me
Feeling me
At all angles
At all ends
There is then
No side
Just you and me
Without sides
Immersed in each other
When all sides disappear
And we are just one
Without a side.

THE PRESENCE

The presence
Is a feeling
That tells me
You are near
Even when you are far
I feel you
Your touch
Your sensation
Your thoughts
From a distance
Physical is an illusion
Presence is felt
When thoughts feel
It is a feeling
That stays with you
All the time
'Til death
That you are with me
Beyond life
Always present.

THE SHEETS

The sheets
If they could talk
They will tell
Stories
About our love
And our lovemaking
How we groped
And explored
Each other
From top to bottom
And everything
In between

The lying down
Feeling the softness of the sheets
The ruffling movements
The shuffling bodies
Reaching for each other
Turning over on our sides
Facing each other
Adjusting our arms
Our bodies
'Til we are body locked
In an embrace
That places our lips
Next to each other
Hungrily searching for each other

They kiss
They lock in an eternal embrace
Exploring

Each other's wet mouths
Tongues lashing out
To elicit
Every sweet nectar

Absorbing flavors
Sweet and godly
Probing its depths
To reach the mind
To tell you
I am yours
You are mine

I want you
You want me

As our arms tighten around us
Pulling us closer
'Til there is no air
Between us
Just two bodies
Glued to each other
Penetrating
Each other's depths
To find comfort
That lies within us

Our bodies struggle
Grapple
Twist and turn
'Til we are locked from top to bottom
In each other
Trying to release the tension
Searching for serenity
That lies within us

Creating movements
Like the rhythms of the waves
Rising to meet the next wave
Undulating like a pendulum
Rocking to and forth
Waiting for the big wave
Its onslaught
Its fury
Its passion
Matching it
With determined force
To tear apart the water
With our own fury, passion and love

The words come in spurts
Whispering
Everlasting love
As our bodies
Continue
Intertwining
Tightening our hold
To never let it go

Movements
Synchronizing
With our breaths
Never separating our mouths
Never leaving our interlocked thighs
Our bodies inside each other
Releasing the nectar of life
That fills both of us
In a sweep

Just as Tsunami hits us
With gigantic force
Expending our energies
Into each other
Washing us
Devoid of life
Listless, spent
Contented, peaceful
Unified, one, immersed, souled
Sharing specks of life
That may ignite
Other life

The waves
Retreating
Leaving us
Together and one
Still immersed and joined
To rest in each other's arms
Quietly and gently
Fulfilled and filled

On the sheets

THE TOUCH

The gentle touch
Caressing
Tingling of fingers
Twining of fingers
Clasping of hands
Shudders a sensation
That vibrates
The entire body
Sending feelings
That arouse emotions
To hold you
To embrace you
Gently but firmly
Letting bodies touch
And explore each other
Seeking unity of emotions
Engulfing passions
To fire our bodies
Into an eternal fire
Of merging souls

It was just a beginning
It was just a touch
The touch

THE LAST LAP

I am running
The last lap
Tired but determined
To not just complete it
For that I will
But with a victory
With my arms raised high
In thrill and exaltation
The cheering of crowds
The glory of the crown
That will be put on my head
I will bow gracefully
With humility
And reflect
On how I got there
Hard work
Determination
Perseverance
Endurance
The grinding of life
The mashing of stones
That crumbles us
Into sand like pieces
That may scatter
In the wind
But those specs
Are alive
They gather
Become a stone
Then a rock
A force
That hits hard
To shake the world

The ashes become a sphinx
Rising
To demonstrate
That there is still
Life left in me
That can
Take on any challenge
That fate hurls at me
I may be on
The last leg of life's journey
But there is still
Life left in me
A burst of energy
A desire to win
I will defeat life
Rise to the occasion
Take on the final challenge
I ran hard
I ran determined
Soon
The wind is behind me
Pushing me, driving me
I gain speed
I pass others
I am at the end
Winning
My hands rise in salute
I win
My life was not in vain
In the end I prevailed
It was the last lap
The final lap of life.

MY ANCHOR

The ship
Has an anchor
It lowers
To stabilize
We as humans
Need an anchor
That keeps us
On track of life.

I have an anchor,
My beloved,
That holds me in place
Stabilizes me
So I don't
Wander in wayward seas
She keeps me
In a direction
That is calm, gentle and soothing
I am at peace
With the world and myself
The reward of emotional stability
She is there
Solid as steel
With a gentle embrace
That holds me to me
Protects me from myself
And keeps me in place
She is my anchor
She is my beloved.

LOST MY CHANCE

I had it
Within my grasp
Just like sand pebbles
Heavy and soft
In my palm
I squeezed it
To hold on
Tight as I can
They oozed out of my hand
Between fingers
'Til all I had
Was few specs
In my palm
The remnants
Of a wasted life
To remind me
That once I had it all
And now
I just have a few specs
Of memories
To last a lifetime.

LOVE OF MY LIFE

The first time
I saw you
You wore green
Slim and elegant
With flowing hair
Long, soft and gentle
Our ride was smooth
The dinner was delicious
A gentle touch
The rubbing of legs
Exciting feelings
Of longing
The talk
Touching of hands
Not letting it go
The sweet smell
Of lips
That reached for each other
It just happened
The caressing of lips
The sweet smell of tongues
Passed an electricity
That told us
That we are in love
We are one
The quiet embrace
The flowing of emotions
Letting life
Guide us
Plunging us
In the hands of God
To hold
And tie our souls

Into one soul
The united soul
The love of my life
Which you are
And will remain
Forever.

THE FUTURE IS THE PAST

What is future?
Reliving of the past
The past that never happened
Or the future
That I want to happen
The dreams
Of the past
Hunting visions
Of an incomplete life
That future
Must satisfy
Correct our past
And make us whole
Whole for our soul
In which
The past is replaced
By future
An unknown world
That fill our past
With grander visions.

I AM BACK

I am back
I was pushed away
But, I came back
I was trampled
I came back
I was slain
I came back alive
The fatal thrusts of life
Failed to annihilate me
They cripple me
But do not end me
The remnants that remain
Group together
Form a force
That pulls me
To new heights
Telling me
It is not over
I am alive
Ready to take on the world
I am back.

SUFFERING FROM MYSELF

I have a fatal disease
I suffer from myself
A disease
That will eventually
Kill me
My follies
My errors
My misjudgments
All piled up
To create a suffering
That I endure
Through life
No cure
Just a bystander
Who sees his own
Suffering
Through his eyes
Not capable
Of curing myself
'Til life
Itself
Becomes the cure.

TOUCHING HAPPINESS

I touch happiness
It feels clear
I grasp
It is empty
I reach
It moves
I lurch
It escapes
It is there
I sense it
It is clear as glass
I feel its presence
But, I can see through it
I touch again
It is cold
Slimy and slippery
Just on the other side
Waiting for me
I feel good
I sensed it
I touched happiness.

A BROKEN VESSEL

A broken vessel
Is a broken vessel
No matter how hard
You may try to repair it
It is fixed
But still broken
You may not see
The cracks
But they still exist
Beneath the surface
Ready to erupt
At any time
To explore the flaws
That hides it
It holds water
But slowly leaks
You patch
The oozing continues
'Til it creates
An ocean
That fills and
Shatters the vessel.

THE BOOK OF MISTAKES

I am an author
I write about my life
A book about my life
A book of mistakes.

Where do I start?
From the beginning
Yes, it began
With a mistake
I was born
At the wrong time
In the wrong place
It had begun
My journey of mistakes
One mistake after another
The wrong career
The wrong loves
The wrong journey
Throwing obstacles
In my path
Every step
A mistake
To remind me
That I was myself
A mistake
Of God
Of life
To teach a lesson
To the world
That what a mistake looks like

So I write
About my life
About my mistakes
Creating
A book of mistakes.

THE LOVE FEAST

The last night
We were together
Was a night to remember
Engraved in our memories
Forever

It was a night
When love blossomed
Passions bloomed
Senses peaked
Bodies
Gorged on each other
Feasting with pleasure
Each other's flesh
Devouring skin
Exploring each orifice
To savor
Every delight
To taste
Every scent

It was
The feast of love
Tasting
Every sensuous sensation
Every quiver of the flesh
Nothing was enough
The night would last forever
The lips locked
In sweet embrace
Sucking sweet nectar.

The tongues
Intertwined with each other
Making passionate love
Pushing, pulling and sucking.
Trying to plunge
Into the soul.

The hands
The tongue
Caressing the body
Gently and firmly
Spreading all over
Feeling each wave
Skin
Cupping the breast
In loving embrace
'Til the hardness of nipples
Invited the mouth
To suck like a baby
Thirsty for milk
To flow out of the breast
Into the thirsty mouth
As your hands
Explore the hardness
That is ready
To erupt
Like a volcano
Ready to squirt
Its hot juices
All over your body.

But the feast has just begun
As bodies
Hungrily attack each other

Sucking life out of
Every orifice
Every hole
'Til there is nothing else to eat
The lips sucking
Every sweetness
From your nest
While your lips
Gently suck
Every part of my body.

'Til there is nothing else
To eat
And then we plunge
Into each other
With such ferocity
To eat
Every morsel
Of sensuous love
Moving in every shape
Every dance
Trying to find
Movements
That don't even exist
Arms entwined
Lips locked
The bodies immersed
In eternal embrace
Not letting go of each other
Not letting the moment end.

It is the last night
The final night
When bodies
Become
One soul

An inseparable soul
Engulfed in each other
Moving gently
And harshly
Thrusting
Receding
Plunging
Trying to find openings
That do not even exist
Quivering with passion
The crescendo of music
Reaching its peak
'Til it erupted
To the joys of the soul
To the joy of the gods
Into a sweet bliss
Creating
A mark on our souls
For in one moment
We merged into each other
Inseparable forever
All inhibitions gone

We were one
Completely one
One soul
That would
Forever
Remain one
As our juices
Flow into each other
To remain there
As part of our blood
To become one
Throughout eternity
Entwined forever

As the night ends
The rays of the sun
Create dawn
The bodies spent
Still intertwined
Lying in
A state of meditation
Peaceful and at bliss.

We have become one
Our hearts are now one
Our sensations are one.

We part
But cannot part
Our senses have become one
Our scents have become one
We are now one
Throughout this life
And throughout eternity
It is the last night
It is the feast of love
We have eating everything
We are full and satisfied
And in God's Hand
It is truly
The love feast.

THE FEAST OF LOVE

There comes a day
In one's life
When love
Becomes a delicacy
It takes over the entire body
You feel love
From head to toe
Full of emotions
Passion and sensuousness
It oozes out of the body
It creates a feast
That will be remembered
Forever.

That one evening
That one night
That lasts forever
It is
The feast of love
The feast to remember

It starts with gentle music
Soft candles
With the scent of
Flowers and incense
Aromating the atmosphere.

The slow dance
The tender touching of bodies
Arms slowly encircling
Each other
The breast
Against the chest

The thighs
Against thighs
The tender caressing
Of backs
The soft kisses
On the cheeks
As passions rise
The lips touch
Creating a tingle
The reverberates
Throughout the body
The embrace tightens
The mouths open
Sensing the scent
Of tongues
As they explore
Each other's mouths
The bodies grinding
Getting hard and moist
As hands roam
Pulling each other
Trying to break
The membrane
Of clothing
Wanting to feel
Flesh
As clothes shed
From top to bottom
The touch of nipples
On chest
Sends lightening
Throughout the body
The hardness
Cupped by thighs

The tip
Rubbing the moistness
As passions grow
The bodies
Tumble to the floor
'Til in an embrace
Bodies locked
As senses erupt
The hands
Spread all over the body
The tongues
Wanting to taste
Every morsel of flesh
Sucking
Ears, neck
Chest, breast
Nipples
Biting and sucking
As mouths
Hungrily travel down
Sucking and eating
The life-givers
As bodies
Go into convulsions
The feast has begun
As we suck
Every juice out of each other
But the hunger
Has just begun
The body wants more
As tongues
Explore every crevice
Trying to suck
Every oyster
Wrapped a pearl

The inflamed bodies
The interlocked tongues
As mouths make
Love to each other
The tongues
Locked in sweet embrace
The bodies
Grinding rhythmically
To find spaces
That don't exist
And naturally
The bodies find
The depths
Which are their homes
Places to nest
And find peace
The main course is here
The love smells
The aroma
The savoring of taste
The bodies know
It is the last night
A night when
Every inhibition
Is thrown away
The bodies want
To merge with
Each other
Become one
Forever.

The bodies are
Fully immersed
Moving and pushing
Shoving and pulling

As they find
Holes
That will give them peace
A home
Where they can
Lie in quietness
Completely
Oblivious of the world
But the passions
Are aroused
The bodies want
To move
But love
Wants to rest
As bodies turn
In different directions
Top to bottom
Bottom to bottom
Top to top
Plunging and exploring
Eating and sucking
'Til the right
Food is sought.

The devouring begins
The gorging begins
You eat, you eat
You plunge and plunge
The bodies
Engorged, immersed
As passions erupt
The embrace tightens
The bodies intertwine
And shudder with joy
As all that we have
Is now satisfied.

But the feast
Does not end
The sensations
Have become inflamed passions
As love, passion and senses
Form their own juice
A new scent
A new aroma
That is us
As evening becomes night
As night goes on
Not wanting the dawn to come
The bodies exhausted
And alive
Not giving up moving
Wanting to squirt
Whatever is still left
The romance
Does not want to extricate
The hunger
Is not over
The feast of love
Goes on
As bodies
Refuse to part
There is still
Life left
The passions are aroused
This time
It is tender
Gentle and loving
Savoring the taste
Smelling the aroma

Inciting emotions
That just don't
Want to give up
But consume
Every food
That left untouched
The exhausted bodies
Find new positions
New movements
Smelling new juices
The earth underneath
Shuddering
Getting heated
As lava boils
Ready to erupt
As bodies squirt
Over each other
Lunge into each other
Erupting with hotness
Every fluid that existed
'Til there is nothing
To come out
The feast is over
Bodies satisfied
Love fulfilled
It is truly
A feast of love.

THE DEMONS INSIDE ME

The demons
Inside me
Clawing
Scrapping
Awakening thoughts
That I am
A failure
A loser
I lost in love
I lost in life
I lost in career
I lost in friendships
But I don't believe it.

I am not a loser
I don't give up
I can't
That would be
Surrendering
I can't do that
For I still love
Desire for love
Lust for life
Dream to succeed
The punching I get
From fate
Cannot let my dreams fade
The dreams are there
They are the past
I can't change that

The past dreams
Become demons
That haunt me
That taunt me
That future
Is not for me
But, I can't accept that
The future is me
The past is past
It cannot control me
The future is free
It has no demons
The demons will lose
As they always do
They should
Life moves forward
Built on love
Built on hope
Built on faith
The demons lose
Life wins.

DARE TO DREAM

I dream
When I am awake
I dream
When I am asleep
I dream
Of a life
That I should have
I dream
Of a life
That I deserve
I dream
Of a love
That I should have.

But, then
Dreams are dreams
Do they come true?
I don't know.
But, dreams are fun
They give you comfort
Hope for the future
Maybe, some of them
Will come true
That will be good
Dreams are us
We must dream
For without dreams
We are empty shells
Just caricatures
Dreams make us humans
They propel us forward
We must not give up

Dreams can become reality
They do
Dream
Dare to dream.

KISMET IS DEAD

Something happened
As I was traveling
Through life
My kismet died
I was left deserted
Left for dead
By fate
Alone to fend for myself
In a marketplace
Where I did not belong
So many people
Yet no one knows me
So many goods
Yet nothing I can afford
I search
For someone I know
But no one is there
I search for my fate
But in the crowd
It is lost
What should I do?
I bump into
Throngs of crowds
Pushed and shoved
I realize that
That this is not my place
I am alone in a crowd
Abandoned by fate
No more kismet
Kismet is dead.

THE GRIND OF LIFE

Life grinds you
Mashes you
Into tiny grains
That slip through your hands
And fall
Squandered
Over a cruel earth
Where people
Walk over you
Crushing
'Til nothing exists
Just a memory
Of a faint existence
That will soon
Evaporate
Into the air
Without a trace.

SELLING THE SOUL

I had a soul
That I sold
For a pittance
To live
In a materialistic world
Where only money matters
Everything has
A monetary value
Even life
Even values
Even souls
Us humans too
We think
Of self-interest first
And what is in it for me today
We sell our souls
Everyday
For instant gratification
For selfish motives
The soul becomes a commodity
To be bought and sold
Just like
Goods in a marketplace
The divine soul
Is just a good
With a price
The decline of humankind
Like a sunset
As the sun
Is swallowed
By the sea.

THE ROBOTIC LIFE

We wake up
Go to work
Do our job
Return home
Do our routines
Watch television
Spend time with family or friends
Eat and sleep
To start the routine
Yes, we have our hobbies
Our interests
We have vacations
We attend parties
And then
All that becomes
A routine
A habit
Just like a robot
Living a robotic life.

TOGETHER YET ALONE

Somewhere out there
Is a person I love
She knows I love her
I know she loves me
Our hearts are one
We are together
But alone
The distance between us
Is too far
That cannot be overcome
But longings and desires
Brings us together
Yet separates us
We are together
In one sense
But may remain
Apart forever.

THE DYING BREED

Once, there were humans
With values
With integrity
With compassion
Who believed
That future would be bright
The youngsters
Will live in a better world
But that hope
Has become a dream
A dream
That will never be realized
The collapse of
Values, integrity, honesty, compassion
Is upon us
We, some humans
Believed in it
But we are
A dying breed.

THE BROKEN HEART

The broken heart
Is a precious ornament
That should hang
From the top of the tallest tree
Radiating love
With brilliant colors
That spread
Throughout the universe
It is a heart
That knows love
That loves
Does not worry
About the consequences
It followed its heart
It wanted to love
Love is eternal
It felt the pang
It felt the pain
It is seasoned
Cultured
Experienced
It is a heart
That grows
That grows into a
Beautiful tree
That gives
Shade, fruits and flowers
Beautifies the world
And plants seeds
For new trees
Love it
Cherish it
The broken heart.

THE FINAL SPARK

The candle flickers
Emitting
Bright colors
As it shines to die
A spark of death
Glowing with pride
As it
Extinguishes itself
To emit
A final glow
'Til there is
No more light
No more heat
The peaceful end
To a burning life.

THE EMOTIONAL RAPE

She loved me
She raped me
She violated my mind
She played with me
I was a toy
That a child loves
Plays with it
Kicks it
Misses it
'Til the child outgrows it
Soon the toy has
No delight
No pleasure
It is discarded
Into a bin
Of discarded toys
The emotional rape.

LIFE LEFT IN ME

There is still life
Left in me
I am still alive
Not dead yet
I can still make it
There is still a
Spark
That will ignite
And light the world
And brighten
The lives of many
It is not the end
But the beginning
A new life
A life
I will be proud of
A life
That will make a difference.

THE OTHER SIDE OF LOVE

There is a side of love
That we don't know
It is not love
It is the opposite of love
When love
Becomes hate
The emotions
Expose
A dark side
Of us
When love
Does not believe in love
When love has left love
Only emptiness remains.

THE LUCKLESS LUCK

I was lucky
That's what I thought
Wonderful parents
Plenty of love
The future was mine.

Then came a storm
I was left alone
To withstand
The blows of life
I did well
I became
A punching bag
I loved
I lose
I was happy
I was sad
I was up
I was down
I was propped up
I was knocked down
I rose
I fell
It just goes on
The undulating waves
With peaks and valleys
Tossing me
Rocking me
Just like my life
With luck
Without luck

To the point
I don't even know
What is luck
If there is
Such a thing
Like luck.

THE MIND OF A TERRORIST

The mind of a terrorist
Is a warped mind
That is full of hatred
Against the world
And against oneself
It was a heart
That no longer exists
To be replaced
By a lump of stone
That is inert
Hard and cruel
Any man, woman or child
In the name of a cause
Calling them revolutionaries
Blaming the world
For their woes
Justifying their actions
For the good of the earth
To them
Killing is the only resort
To their hatred
Of themselves
Dialogue and compassion
Are out
Programmed from childhood
By elders
Who themselves
Led a depraved life
Breeding hatred
Rather than love

In the young minds
Pure and innocent
To corrupt them
Depriving them
Of a life
They are destined to lead
A life of goodwill, love and happiness
Family and children
Killing them
In their prime
Without a life
Is cruelty beyond cruelty
Against God's works
Against God's words
It is against God
The mind of a terrorist.

LOVE AMONG THE RUINS

The ruins
Of an ancient civilization
Are the best places
For love
Just like
A radiant flower
In the wilderness
Beautifies the forest
Love blossoms
The lonely life
Even if it does
For a short time
It gives life
To a dead soul
Love is
And should remain
Among the ruins.

THE CURSE OF THE PAST

I am cursed
By my past
The things I did
The people I hurt
The mistakes I made
I am haunted
By those curses
That eat into me
Gnawing at my soul
Tormenting with temptations
To lead me astray
I fend off the curse
With all my might
To fall into a vise
That squeezes me
To extract every ounce of blood
That is left in me
It is the curse of my past.

THE HEART AND ME

My heart and I
Don't get along
I don't listen to it
For it prompts me with truth
About me
I don't like to hear
My heart tells me
What I should do
Even if it hurts
I choose the easy path
Ignore the heart
And pay the price.

MY LUCK

My luck and I
Are aliens
When I want it
It deserts me
When I don't want it
It bails me out
We are never together
We are there
But not with each other
We are thrown together
We have learned to adjust
But not really loving
We just don't see eye to eye
But it is there
Whatever it is
My luck.

WITHOUT LOVE

Without love
Life could be simple
But not worth living
It would be painless
But not pleasurable
I may be happy
And alone
But not contented
And full
It will be life
Just an ordinary life
Not a life
Worth living
Life
Without love.

A PERFECT LOSER

I love to lose
I have perfected the game
Of losing
I create ways
To lose
Ways that hurt me
But that hurt
Gives me pleasure
As pain and pleasure
Go together
I lose in love
In life
But I try again
To lose again
The game goes on
Making me
A perfect loser.

I FEEL UNCLEAN

I feel unclean
I need to wash
Wash away
The false promise of love
Wash away
The deceitful embraces
The pretense of hope
The lies of the heart
I am covered
With the slime
Of unholy mud
That suffocates my skin
Breathing life
Out of my blood
To wash the slime
Of cruel humans
Who prey on the innocent
To suck every follicle of skin
To breed on their
Lust of destruction
Against innocence
Spreading cruelty
On the mind
Creating bitterness
And negativeness
But it must be washed
Washed with ferocity
To remove
Every dirt
Every grain of unclean sand
'Til the skin can breathe
Breathe the purity
Of life and love.

SELF-INFLICTED WOUNDS

My body
Is covered
With self-inflicting wounds
The scars I carved myself
On my innocent body
Which was clean and pure
Now it is scared and ugly
Reminding me
Of the monument of mistakes
That I erected
Over a damaged soul
I am entombed
In my own body
Covered with
Lessons of life
Of self-inflicting blows.

THE DIVINE BLOWS

The divine blows
Come in all shapes and sizes
From the gentle nudge
To a hammer on the head
Each blow is a lesson
A lesson
That I am not listening
To myself
The voice inside me
The routine of life
Turns humans into animals
Living each day
Without a purpose
And then the blows come
The divine guidance
That tells us
We have lost God.

I AM NOT THE RIGHT PERSON

I am not
The right person
For this world
As I walk through the streets
I feel alien
I see people shopping
For goods and services
For instant gratification
When I search for
Values and integrity
That underlies
The foundation of
A decent society
I see materialism and selfishness
What is good for me today
Who cares for the future
The future is away
I want to live today
I see shoppers
Adoring goods
That make them look good
But their souls are empty
For there are
No goods for the soul
Just emptiness
Empty stares
I seek salespeople
I walk around
Hoping to see
A soul
But all I see
Are shoppers

Who enjoy shopping
But not the buying
I am searching
For true honest goods
I can't find them
What I find
I touch
And they vanish at my touch
I gaze at empty space
But I am alone
People are pushing and shoving
But I don't feel it
I walk through the crowds
But can't see them
Soon I am out
Standing at the wilderness
Free and fresh
Then I realize
I am not the right person
For this life
For this world.

THE PRISONER OF SELF

I am a prisoner
Of myself

I want to do
What I should
But, I don't
Something holds me
I don't know
Why, I don't know
I want to break out
But I am tied
In a straight jacket
I want to write
To express myself
But, I can't
My tongue is tied
My hands cannot move
I struggle
To break free
My mind and my heart
Embrace to break
Away from each other
They need each other
The struggle goes on
The birds fly
Free anywhere
My life does
Want to be free
Fly, soar
But, I am held
By gravity
Holding me

To live life
That I don't want
I am a prisoner
Of myself.

RICH AND POOR

Why some are rich
And, why some are poor
Is it fate?
While some are born into wealth
While some struggle their entire life
Is it all about money?
The rich live a comfortable life
While poor exist day to day
Does it mean
That rich are virtuous
And poor are sinners
Why did God
Make it such
The rich offer charities
To help the poor
But, charity is charity
What can the poor
Offer the rich
An appreciation of life
An understanding of survival
The art of survival
Or, an insight into
The realities of life
Will the rich learn
Checkbook generosity
An ancient ritual
To keep the poor quiet
But, rich are not rich
Poor are not poor
It is all relative.

THE TEMPLE OF SINS

I have erected
A beautiful temple
That enshrines
My sins
To create
An aura
Of imperfection
A simple human
Who failed to understand life
And let emotions guide him
Committing sins
That soon became a temple
Where I worship
The lost life
That I ruined
By my sins
Sins that I thought
Were not sins
Love honestly
Be honest
Show integrity
Care for people
Impart wisdom
But then
I was wrong
They turned out
To be sins
Love was abused
Honesty was not a virtue
Integrity was not a virtue
Caring meant hurt

Being nice
Meant weakness
Meant dullness
So, let these be my sins
I did them all
Now I stand alone
In this sacred temple
That is holy and spiritual
It is my temple
It is me.

I MISS LIFE

Some time ago
My life left me
Left me alive
To face the struggles
And emotional upheavals
I am alone
Wondering what to do
I have no one
To turn to
No one to learn from
I know my life and I
Did not always get along
But, it was part of me
I grew up with it
It would guide me
Share my experiences
Teach me lessons
Now I am lost
No one to guide me
No one to share my experiences
I have to fend for myself
I wish
Life were here
To hold my hand
But, I have to learn
To be alone
Without life
Living a life
Without life.

AS TIME GOES BY

As time goes by
It becomes cruel
And a blessing
The friends that we grew up with
Become strangers
Not necessarily by choice
Some by distance
Some by marriage
Some by life
Some by wisdom
Interests change
Lifestyles change
We still keep in touch
With some childhood friends
Not for friendship
More for nostalgia
To reflect on
The good old days
That makes us feel good.

But, time has passed
We are in different time zones
The world is same or new
Depends on how you look at it
We have new friends
More for socializing
Than for soul-searching
The truth of the past
Is replaced by
Artificiality of belonging
Priorities change
We are no longer
On the list of calls
Our thinking has changed

Loneliness
Wants friendships
That are no longer there
It is best
To reflect on the good times
Fond memories
Happy events
And bury them
In the heart
And move on
With a smile
On our lips
The past is over
Time has passed
And it is
A new time.

A LOVELESS LIFE

A loveless life
Is a sacred life
An empty vessel
Waiting to be filled
With the elixir of love
Ready to accept
The divine spirit
But the hollow shell
Rings a bell
That it shall remain empty
There is nothing to fill
The vessel must endure
A vacuum
Just waiting
Just wanting
Like a loveless life.

THE FABRIC OF THE HEART

The fabric of the heart
Is weak
Gentle and fragile
It can only hold so much
Before it crumbles.

It is woven
To gently hold love
Give it warmth
Nurture it
And keep it dry.

But, love is unpredictable
The heart becomes heavy
Covered with tears
'Til the fabric cannot hold it
It is stretched
It breaks
The fabric
Is no longer a fabric.

LET THE TORCH PASS

There comes a time
In one's life
When the torch is passed
To the next generation
And we must fade into oblivion
We create
A next generation
We must prepare
Them for the future
It is our responsibility
It is the evolution of life
As our lives
Sees the sunset
We see
The sunrise of the next generation
The torch passes
We feel pride
In what they do in their future
We have done what we have done
It is past
The future is theirs
We are the past
Life moves forward
The torch passes
We must give it
The brightest light.

THE LONE RANGER

The lone ranger
Takes on the world by himself
Alone against the cruel world.

Many times in our life
We are like
Lone rangers
Fighting demons
That we must
To find a life
That we must
Like a lone ranger.

THE DISEASE OF LONELINESS

Loneliness is a disease
That affects us
Once in a while
When we feel
There is no one there for us
We are alone
In this universe
Fighting the cruel world
Like a lone ranger
But, we are never alone
There is someone
Watching over us
God
We do not see
But God is there
With love and protection
We may not feel
We may feel desolate
But, we are not alone
We are alive
Life may not be what we want
But, life is life
What is fair
By what standard
Where there is no standard in life
All life is relative
People are people
Absorbed in themselves
Only there
When self-interest prevails
We are always alone
From birth to death

But, loneliness is self-defeating
It is a disease that we must avoid
And give ourselves
To the hand of God.

THE LOSER'S PARADISE

The losers in life
Do have a paradise
Which they share
With other losers
To share their stories
Of life and love
The hurts and pains
That permeates
The soul
To reflect on
Why we lose?
Is it us?
Or, is it luck?
Maybe both
But losers
Learn a lesson
That life is not fair
We are all losers
In some aspect of life
The paradise
Is within us
Which we have abandoned
We have separated us from us
And plunged us into a world
A collection of losers
Where past is king
And future is not there
It is the loser's paradise.

BROKEN PROMISES

Broken promises
Are like
A broken vase
That maybe put together
But, it is not the same
It has cracks
Though sealed
Vulnerable and fragile
To be held gently
Afraid that
The next fall
Will shatter it to pieces
Pieces that will disintegrate
Into the earth
Leaving an empty space
Where broken promises
Reside.

THE WRONG TRAIN

I had to make a journey
A journey of life
I arrive at the station
Ask the conductor
For the right train
I know my destination
I board the train
The journey starts
I see fellow travelers
All around me
The train gallops
And soon
The past is gone
The future comes
Bearing down on you
The station comes
It doesn't look familiar
You were on the wrong train
You trusted the conductor
What do you do?
You search the faces
Of fellow travelers
Some smile, some frown
Some turn away
Who do you ask?
You trust Fate
Maybe, the new destination
Is the right one
Or should you go to the next station
And find another train
But, how do you know
That the next station
Is the right place to step down

Maybe, the trains there
Take you in another direction
You sit, you wait
The train thunders on
You are surrounded by strangers
All cheering your wasteful journey
The end comes, you are there
The destination, not what you wanted
But, it is home
The price of the wrong train.

THE CROSSROADS OF LIFE

The crossroads
Of life
Make you wonder
Where to go?
The paths all look the same
But, they lead to different places
You cannot see the end
But, you must take the path
Life is always at crossroads
You are making choices
At every step
Some wise
Some foolish
But those are our choices
They determine our journey
We are forever
At the crossroads.

THE CORRUPTED MIND

The mind

The thinking soul
Gets corrupted
By what it sees in this world
The glorifying of wealth
As the means to everything
Selling us mentally and physically
To maintain an existence
'Til death eventually embraces us.

The mind
That gives up thinking
To embrace
The words and opinions
Of others
Forsaking its own thinking
To live an easy life
Why think?
When others can do it for you
An easy way to live
We become a zombie
The brain is not ours anymore
It is our brain
But the thoughts are others
We are no longer ourselves
Just cogs in a wheel
That turns us
When the wheels turn
We are corrupted
Our minds are corrupted
We are all

Empty

THE LOST SOUL

Somewhere
Sometime ago
I lost touch with myself
When that happened
I don't know
Why it happened
I don't know
But, I broke away from myself
My body went one way
My soul went one way
Once together
We split
And now
We search for each other
In the wilderness of the world
Among lost humanity
Among the ruins
Of values and integrity
But we need each other
To be one
Living in harmony
And fight the onslaughts
Of the cruel world
I need my soul
My soul needs me
It needs a place
To reside
I need the wisdom
Of the wise.

MY MIND IS MY ENEMY

I have
A wonderful mind
Smart and alert
Too smart at times
It takes over
Justifies everything
It wants to do
Overriding my heart
And clouding my emotions
With logic
Ignoring my inner voice
I listen to it
For it makes sense
It ignores the reality
It may be right
But, it is also
My enemy.

I AM AN ISLAND

I am an island
A small piece of deserted land
Somewhere in the middle
Of a vast ocean
So much water
No land in sight.
I sit there alone
Surviving with few trees
That occasionally
Drop some fruit and leaves
To make me feel
Inhabited.
Once, I was part of a land
That flourished with life
Then a jolt happened
That split me
While savage waves
Pounded me
And buried me
With water
And when I emerged
I realized
I was alone
Staring
At the vast expanse of water
That suddenly surrounded me
As I wait
To be discovered
To show the world
That I am ancient
A relic
A piece of the past
Waiting for the future.

THE WOUNDS OF LOVE

The wounds of love
Are precious
They should be
Nurtured
And treated with
Love and tenderness
For these wounds are
Divine
A gift of God
That tells us
That we can love
And we are not
Afraid to get hurt
The feeling of love
Is God
Cherish it
Respect it
And thank God
For having it.

OVERCOMING MYSELF

I am
My worst enemy
I set goals
I don't make them
I make resolutions
Which I break right away
I make decisions
That I justify being right
Then I lament
That those were mistakes
This cycle continues
I have to overcome myself
For I am my worst enemy.

THE BROKEN HOPE

I had hopes
Of myself
From friends and relatives
From the world
But those hopes
Dashed against the wall
Likes waves
Crashing on the rock
And splintering
In small particles in all directions
As nothing is left.

My hopes
Of a great life
Shattered
As the world
Grinds them
Into the sand
To let people
Trample on them
And walk away
Without thinking
That they just
Stepped on hope
And crushed it to bits.
It lies there
Crushed
But not dead
Alive
In its own hope
For even
Hope has hope
'Til it is broken again
To rise again.

LIFE ENDS

When does life end?
The obvious answer is
At death.
But, that is not true
For life can end
Many times
Before death.
It ends
When you stop dreaming
It ends
When you lose faith
It ends
When you stop
Living for life
And retire to
Just an existence
Just a survival
We lie to ourselves
For we have to live
Smell the flowers
For that's all there is left
Our life ended
Some time ago
When we let it end
In the middle of life
When we let it go
For in reality
Life never ends
It is up to you
For only you can end life
Not death
For death is divine

But you are human
And humans control their destiny
Life is precious
It is personal
And you must live it
Only you can do it
Life is life
You make it
You break it
It is your life
You are the Creator
You are Divine.

THE END OF AN AFFAIR

The end of an affair
Is an occasion
To celebrate
Love
For you loved
You were able to love
That is a gift
But, that does not mean
That love finds happiness
Maybe, it is not meant to be
It is over
You are richer
You are loved
Love resides in you
The affair may be over
But love remains
In you.

THE VANISHING INTELLECT

What is intelligence?
The human advantage
That separates
Humans from beasts
We strive for
Mediocrity
Why think?
When other can do it for us
Instead of health gyms
We need
Intelligence clubs
Where people can exchange
Ideas and beliefs
And not kill each other
In the process
The human value
The power of the mind
Is being eroded
By media and pundits
Who banish our thinking
To replace it with
Opinions that are not ours
We lose the ability
To think on our own
Why not?
When we let
Others think for us
And make us into
Robots and zombies
That live
Day by day
Paycheck to paycheck
Hoping
That our dreams will come true
When our dreams
Are controlled by others
Because
We have left our intellect to others

ABOUT THE AUTHOR

Dan Khanna considers himself a traveler through life enjoying an adventurous journey.

Dan was born in New Delhi, India. After he completed high school at St. Columbus High School, Dan left India striking out for California via short stays in London, Montreal and Milwaukee, Wisconsin. Although his dream was to pursue a career in the arts, acting, music, and writing, a quirk of fate placed him in engineering college and pursuing a business management career, in which he excelled. Dan completed an undergraduate program in engineering, and a Master and Doctorate in Business Administration.

Dan worked in Silicon Valley's high technology firms and was a CEO and founder of several firms. He changed careers to be a professor. Now, he again is pursuing his dream in creative endeavors.

Dan is the quintessential Renaissance Man, whose interests span the gamut of the arts, sciences, history, social and political studies, classics and philosophy. His search for knowledge began in his early life where his father was the Chief Education Officer of Delhi and his mother was a Sanskrit scholar. Dan speaks English, Hindi, Urdu, Punjabi, and Gujarati.

As a child, Dan read voraciously, particularly enjoying novels, such as Sherlock Holmes, Agatha Christie, Earl Stanley Gardener, Ian Fleming's James Bond series and classic works of Shakespeare, Tolstoy, Dickens, Oscar Wilde, Thomas Hardy, and other writers. He was very interested in poetry and read English poems of Browning, Keats, Milton, Tennyson, and Frost, as well as, other poets, while mastering Urdu poetry. His intellectual interests including studying Western and Eastern philosophers, especially Socrates, from whom he learned questioning methodology employed in his research, lectures and seminars.

During his parochial education, Dan was interested in various sports: cricket, soccer and field hockey. His love for the arts and music was honed to a level that he performed in plays, movies and solo concerts.

Dan's present journey is devoted to creative arts and activities, primarily writing poetry, fiction and non-fiction books and plays, while continuing to acquire knowledge of diverse subjects. He has published one book and has written over twelve hundred poems comprising eighteen books to date. Dan has several non-fiction and fiction books in development.

www.ingramcontent.com/pod-product-compliance
Lightning Source LLC
Chambersburg PA
CBHW071310060426
42444CB00034B/1767